*Mary,
Thank q
these poes
with others. Doug*

Poetry for the common (Wo)Man

Poetry for the common (Wo)Man

Douglas D. Bruffett

iUniverse, Inc.
New York Lincoln Shanghai

Poetry for the common (Wo)Man

Copyright © 2006 by Douglas D. Bruffett

All rights reserved. No part of this book may be used or reproduced by any means, graphic, electronic, or mechanical, including photocopying, recording, taping or by any information storage retrieval system without the written permission of the publisher except in the case of brief quotations embodied in critical articles and reviews.

iUniverse books may be ordered through booksellers or by contacting:

iUniverse
2021 Pine Lake Road, Suite 100
Lincoln, NE 68512
www.iuniverse.com
1-800-Authors (1-800-288-4677)

ISBN-13: 978-0-595-38535-5 (pbk)
ISBN-13: 978-0-595-82921-7 (cloth)
ISBN-13: 978-0-595-82913-2 (ebk)
ISBN-10: 0-595-38535-4 (pbk)
ISBN-10: 0-595-82921-X (cloth)
ISBN-10: 0-595-82913-9 (ebk)

Printed in the United States of America

Index

Actions	113
Angels Among Us	115
Artist's Eye	117
Artists	9
Attic	119
Beauty	10
Break Up Kit	120
Cancer	68
Cats	12
Chatham	122
Cheat in a small town	125
Chemistry	127
Choices	129
Chosen Memories	130
Clean mind	104
Consumed	133
Control	18
Creativity	102
Dancer (1st version)	85
Dancer (2nd version)	87
Date in a Small Town	131
Dawn	134
Doris	135
Dream	6
Each day's better than the next	137
Eighty Years	69

Eternity	*138*
Etheree of Man	*181*
Etheree to Poetry	*182*
Etherees	*180*
Failure	*109*
First Love	*14*
Five Stages of Grief	*16*
Flags	*19*
Fool	*140*
Forgotten Veteran	*21*
Friend	*3*
Friends	*142*
Garden	*23*
Go Vote	*149*
Gossip	*168*
Gossip	*26*
Haikus	*39*
Honky-tonk toy	*145*
How do you know	*150*
How in the world can I miss you.	*147*
Husband and Wife	*28*
I Love	*30*
I loved her just in time	*152*
I Quit	*32*
I Was There	*153*
I wish upon our star	*157*
I Yearn	*35*
I'll Crawl Through Glass	*36*
I'll wait	*158*
I'm glad that I miss you	*161*
If	*5*
Immortality	*141*
It Didn't Kill Me	*162*

It's Not Called Cheatin' Anymore	37
It's our turn	174
Journey	79
Just Me	41
Keep It Simple Sir (K.I.S.S.)	40
Labor of love	75
Leftover Limericks	199
Lever	2
Life	25
Lillie	45
Limerick of a Hooker	43
Limerick of Paul	72
Limerick of the Lady	179
Limerick of Youth	111
Locker	163
Looks	164
Love	52
Lover's Place	48
Luck	49
Masquerade	156
Maturity	44
Memory	51
Micro-Management	53
Misery	166
Miss Behavin'	59
Mother	56
My Name is Shelia	57
Next	169
No "L"	139
Not easy	93
Obesity	66
October	173
Old Dancer	62

One Sided Love	171
Our Love	65
Outside	176
Personals	73
Pets	11
Phone message	78
Poetry for the Common Man	1
Promises	136
Reducing Poetry	198
Relationships	34
Respect	82
Retired	76
Retirement Community	95
Roses (1st version)	80
Roses (2nd version)	81
Santa Claus	108
Season of Confusion	60
She wants what you have	84
Sick	91
Sister	144
Space	92
Strength	67
Students	175
Success	47
Summer wind	94
Suspenders	177
Teachers	55
Teddy Bear	7
The Country Singer	89
The Editor	106
The Glow	103
The Kiss	112
The Man	195

The Man	*110*
The Test	*178*
The Tomb	*183*
The Voice	*101*
The Wall	*105*
Tomatoes	*100*
Tools	*170*
Trust	*151*
Two Friends	*38*
Vandalism	*61*
Velvet Chain	*154*
Vocabulary	*107*
Vows	*83*
Waitin'	*188*
Wake Up At Six	*159*
Wall of Stone	*185*
Warm On The Outside	*186*
We Need To Talk	*189*
What is this?	*191*
What's the Difference	*192*
Who's the Whore?	*197*
Why must you try to change me?	*193*
Yard Sale	*97*
You're the one I think of	*194*
Young	*196*

Foreword

It is my belief that poetry should be entertaining, inspiring, thought provoking, and comforting. Most importantly, it should rhyme and have a sense of rhythm.

My original purpose in writing poetry was to entertain my family, a few close friends, and myself. Their comments and encouragement led to multiple versions of some poems as well as the publication of this book.

While it is exciting to win awards and have poetry published, the greater reward is to hear of a poem that inspired or comforted someone and realize it is one you wrote.

There was no attempt to organize or categorize this collection. What might appear humorous to one might be perceived as serious by another.

The quotes interspersed throughout this book are original to the best of my knowledge.

Please read the poem on page one. If you agree with its premise, this book might be for you.

Acknowledgement

This collection of poetry could not have been written without the inspiration and support of many people. Some are family, some are friends, others are wives and lovers. They are listed in alphabetical order by first name only. There is no explanation provided as each will know the part they played.

Anita, Belva, Beth, Bill, Bob, Betty, Brent, Cheryl, Christie, Dan, Dave, Daphne, Debbie, Dina, Dixie, Doris, Doug, Ealum, Gary, Gina, James, Jean, Jordan, Joyce, Juanita, Karen, Lee Ann, Leon, Linda, Lou, Maria, Mary, Michelle, Morgan, Nancy, Patsy, Roger, Ronnie, Shelia, Shirley, Steven, Tanner, Tim, Tom, Toni, Vickie, Wanda, Walter, Wendell, Whitney, and Wyatt.

Among those named are two very special ladies who entered my life at an important juncture. They are both artists in their own right. Shirley is an internationally renowned painter and Beth is the most accomplished dancer and sweetest love I have ever known.

Poetry for the Common Man

*It's doubtful I will ever be
a connoisseur of poetry.
I find the haiku much too terse,
and still prefer the rhyming verse.*

*The sonnet with it's rigid rules
seems more adapt for writing schools.
If I must read with reference book
do not expect a second look.*

*I am the one you claim to seek,
and cry because your sales are weak.
I think you're trying way too hard
to ever be the public's bard.*

*If book reviews leave you in tears,
you may be writing to your peers.
Perhaps the secret of success
is know the rules, but use them less.*

Lever

*If there was a lever you could pull,
to make all the jerks disappear,*

*could you approach with confidence,
and pull it without fear?*

Friend

Who answers the phone
in the middle of the night?
With just one concern.
Is everything all right?
Who listens quietly
to what's on your mind,
and reassures you with words
both gentle and kind?

Who do you run to
with something to share,
when you're looking for someone
that you know will care?
Who makes you feel special
when they look at you?
Who takes a real interest
in all that you do?

Who knows all your secrets
and loves you the same?
Who never keeps score,
because it isn't a game?
Who can you turn to
when you just need a smile?
Who can you count on
for that extra mile?

Who laughs when you're happy
and cries when you're sad?
Who shares the good times
as well as the bad?
Who's there to help you
to meet life's demands?
Who lightens your burden
with their willing hands?

*Who do you know
that will help lift you up,
when it's your turn to drink
from life's bitter cup?
Someone you know
who's there 'til the end.
Who do you know,
that you call a friend?*

If

*If I got what I deserve,
two things I know are true.*

*I would not have eternal life,
and I would not have you.*

Dream

To dream, is but to plan with hope.

Teddy Bear

*Was there ever a time
when he wasn't there?
That soft and cuddly
Teddy Bear.
With a gentle smile
who knew what to do.
His arms open wide
with a big hug for you.*

*He held you close
as night time drew near.
He chased away monsters
and quieted your fear.
With ears made for chewing
when first teeth came through.
A trip to the laundry
he was almost like new.*

*When you started walking
he was always in tow.
The miles that you dragged him
no one can know.
If he had rough treatment
it doesn't show.
There are a few places
where fur doesn't grow.*

*You started to school
and began making friends.
You learned what was real,
and where make believe ends.
When you had tea parties,
there was always a chair,
reserved for no other
than your teddy bear.*

*You entered a new age
and put away toys.
You began wearing makeup
and noticing boys.
But your teddy bear
still played a part.
He helped you get over
your first broken heart.*

*When you went to college,
so did your bear.
Others made fun
but you didn't care.
It was the first time
you'd been on your own.
He brought you comfort
when you felt alone.*

*You're all grown up now,
but some things don't change.
When you decorate,
you always arrange,
a place for your memories
for others to share.
And there in the middle
is your teddy bear.*

*Some day you'll cross over
to the sweet by and by.
To spend all eternity
with loved ones on high.
Don't be surprised
if the first angel there,
with arms open wide
is your teddy bear.*

Artists

*An artist has something
which sets them apart.
They can touch with their eyes
and see with their heart.
They look at the world
in a different light.
Perhaps they're the ones
who are seeing things right.*

*An artist is chosen
and called for a task.
Their creator's gift,
which they didn't ask.
They don't have to use it,
but it's always there.
May God bless the ones
who are willing to share.*

*An artist is special,
of that there's no doubt.
But don't even bother
to figure it out.
In this troubled world,
with it's turmoil and strife,
just be ever grateful,
if one's in your life.*

Beauty

I surround myself with beauty
just as I am doing now.
Whether art, or flower, or lady fair,
I'm drawn to it somehow.
I'm not a shallow person,
beauty's not just of the eye.
There's some of it in each of us.
You'll find it, if you try.

It may be something fleeting
they never will repeat.
Perhaps an impish twinkle
every time that your eyes meet.
It could be their attentive ways
or something in their smile.
I only know when I see them,
I'm happy for a while.

There may be something more to it,
not easy to explain.
It's a complicated feeling,
partly joy, partly pain.
As if the very sight of them
just makes you yearn for more,
and leaves a hollow, empty space
when they walk out the door.

If each time you glance at them,
you see them look your way.
You'll know you've caught them taking in
the beauty you display.
So be the person that you are.
There's only one of you.
Reflect God's given beauty
in every thing you do.

Pets

Pets are people, without the faults

Cats

So, you own a cat.
Surely you jest.
They will not allow it.
You feed them at best.
At times they will please you.
More often they'll taunt.
But you can be sure
they'll do what they want.

It's easy to see
that you're not respected.
Perhaps you enjoy
being rejected.
When they want your loving,
they'll come to you.
Until they are ready,
there's naught you can do.

So you own a cat.
An illusion at best.
If you don't agree,
try this simple test.
Who feeds and pampers
and cleans up the mess?
Who lies there watching
and couldn't care less?

They jump on the table
and eat from your plate.
It's not that they think
your food is so great.
They don't think they're human.
It's nothing like that.
They just think that you
are a much larger cat.

*If you seek adoration
or a love that is true,
you should look elsewhere,
a cat's not for you.
If you can get used to
being treated like that,
you'll know the true joy
of feeding a cat.*

First Love

*We were so young
to be on our own.
Yet they dropped us off
and left us alone.
The first time I saw you,
we both were in tears.
You reached for my hand
and quieted my fears.*

*We were both frightened,
but within the hour,
love had us caught up
in it's awesome power.
We counted the minutes
'til school would begin.
Then we'd find each other
and fall over again.*

*Too soon it was Summer
and we had to part.
We each swore our true love
and then crossed our heart.
Your dad got a new job
and took you away.
So you wouldn't be there
on that sad first day.*

*Time may heal wounds,
but still leaves a scar.
My heart is there with you
wherever you are.
I may find a new love,
as this life I live.
But there will be something
that I cannot give.*

*You'll always be there
in the back of my mind.
I pray you'll find someone,
and they'll treat you kind.
They'll never love you
the way that I do.
There's only one first love,
for me it was you.*

Five Stages of Grief

Denial

   *I know he's still talking
but what's being said.
I can't hear a word
for this clock in my head.
This cannot be true.
There's been a mistake.
Is there more he can do?
More tests I can take?*

Anger

   *I don't understand it.
I've always been good.
I shouldn't have cancer.
I know some who should.
Is this how you pay me
for all I have done?
If you're looking for martyrs,
I don't want to be one.*

Bargaining

   *I know I was wrong
to blame this on you.
If you will just cure me,
here's what I will do.
I'll volunteer time
for the shut-ins and poor,
and try to give comfort
to those near death's door.*

Depression

   *Why do you ignore me
when I seek your face?
Am I so unworthy
of your healing grace?
I need you to be here
to help lift me up.
I can't drink alone
from this bitter cup.*

Acceptance

*If this is the plan
you have for me.
I'll bow to your will
and give praises to Thee.
Help me to show others
the blessings you give,
and be your reflection
as long as I live.*

Control

*I can't control your action,
but I can control my reaction.*

Flags

*There are flags for every nation
they unfurl at break of day.
They're used to mark the boundaries
and keep enemies at bay.
If flags lead men in battle,
and are lowered in retreat,
then the sexual revolution flag
must be the toilet seat.*

*You've come a long way baby
since the time you first began.
The law now says a woman
is as good as any man.
Now there is just one difference
that the laws can not allow.
They tell us where we have to go,
but can not tell us how.*

*I think that you should tell me
what the problem really is.
Can't you check to see the seat is down
before you do your biz?
Nature played the trick on you,
don't take it out on me.
You must sit while I can stand
and that's how it will be.*

*Why does it really matter
if the seat is up or down.
It's not like I had planned it
in the hope that you would drown.
The reason that you give me
makes me think you're not so bright.
You hate to sit in water
when you have to go at night.*

*A man can change his ways
if there's a valid reason to.
But I don't think the story
that you're telling me is true.
Just tell me the true reason
why you put on such a show.
Is it because it hurts
that you must sit down when you go?*

Forgotten Veteran

*He drives himself home
this veteran's day.
He works with his hands
and there isn't much pay.
He thinks of his friends
who called him a fool
for serving his country
while they went to school.*

*Now they have their families,
their houses and cars,
while he drowns his memories
in neighborhood bars.
He drags himself home
and lays down his head.
He prays that the dreams
won't come to his bed.*

*He knows all to well
the hatred and horror
of fighting his country's
unpopular war.
He thought it was over
when he got off the plane.
But they spat in his face
and held him to shame.*

*He isn't a hero
nor pretends to be.
Is it asking too much
for others to see?
He was doing his duty,
like his father before.
He just wants respect,
he's not asking for more.*

*When veterans gather
from all the wars past,
is it really too much
for him to ask,
to be included among
those honored ranks,
and receive his nation's
heartfelt thanks.*

*Ronald Lee Bruffett
(April 12, 1946–July 7, 1990)*

Garden

*You came to me
and my barren soil.
Where nothing would flourish,
in spite of my toil.
Your very presence
was all that it took
to transform the garden
like a page in a book.*

*You had what some
would call a green thumb.
But it wasn't your hands
that the beauty came from.
Your heart held the secret
to a beautiful life,
free from the stress
and the turmoil and strife.*

*There was something about you,
that didn't fit in.
A sad, hungry look
crossed your eyes now and then,
like something was calling
to you from afar,
and your heart was tethered
to some distant star.*

*Then one day it happened
and you went away.
You said you'd been happy
but you couldn't stay.
There was something out there
that you didn't know,
but when it called to you,
then you had to go.*

*I come to the garden
where flowers used to grow.
If you've never seen them,
then you wouldn't know,
such beauty existed
and so pleased the eye.
How I envy the roses,
at least they could die.*

Life

*Without love,
life is just a lot of time.*

Gossip

*Beware of the gossip,
it's probably lies,
if you didn't see it
with your own two eyes.
Even then,
it may not be true.
Sometimes your vision
can play tricks on you.*

*Who is the gossip,
and what makes them tick?
They're a little bit jealous,
a little bit sick.
What about us,
who just listen in?
As they cast the stone,
are we without sin?*

*Watch out for small minded
and envious lot.
Their tongues may be bitter,
but that's all they've got.
They seek to destroy
all that you build.
The smile tries to hide it,
the intent is ill willed.*

*The next time you're listening,
ask yourself why,
you don't turn away,
do you even try?
You may think it's funny
when they put me down.
But who is the subject
when you're not around?*

Join them or fight them.
The free will is yours.
But remember that gossips
are audio whores.
They get their pleasure
from other folks pain.
They don't do it for money,
so what is the gain?

Husband and Wife

*We've come here today
to celebrate life.
As <u>Name</u> and <u>Name</u>
become husband and wife.
When two join together,
they build something new.
There now are three people
where once there were two.*

*"Two become one."
I've heard all my life.
But who will survive?
The husband or wife.
It would be better,
so it seems to me,
when two come together,
they then become three.*

*To build the third person,
you each must bring parts.
It goes without saying,
the first are your hearts.
You won't really need them,
'cause after you're done,
within the new person,
two hearts beat as one.*

*Your hands should be added.
It can't be all fun.
You're building a future.
There's work to be done.
It's not always easy.
You'll toil sun to sun.
It will be the best work
that you've ever done.*

Hold back just a little
of when you were two.
It's what makes you special
and why they love you.
No need to surrender
who you really are.
It's those things about you
that brought you this far.

Be there for each other,
but have time alone.
True love does not weaken
when left on it's own.
So now you must choose.
Which one it will be?
Do you become one,
or will it be three?

I Love

*I love the way you look at me,
when others do not see.
With love that spans the distance,
given unconditionally.*

*I love the warmth of your embrace
when music starts to play.
I love to hold you close to me
and feel your body sway.*

*I love the twinkle in your eyes,
the smile upon your face.
I love to hear you whisper low,
"this is my favorite place".*

*I love the way you tease me
with your eyes, your words, your touch,
and knowing when the time is right,
you'll please me just as much.*

*I love the way you come to me
with hungry heart aflame,
and as we melt together,
tenderly call out my name.*

*I love the fire of pure desire
that dances in your eyes,
and as our passion rises,
hear the softness of your sighs.*

*I love the gentle way you touch
with tenderness that says so much.
I love the way you're always there
to show me just how much you care.*

*I love to know that I'm the one
you dream of while you sleep,
and that the heart I gave to you
is safe within your keep.*

*I love the way there's room for me
in everything you do,
and if you haven't guessed by now,
I'm saying "I love you".*

I Quit

*It's business as usual
and how it must be.
I won't hang around
while you replace me.
So I'm giving notice,
consider this is it.
You don't have to fire me,
'cause baby I quit.*

*You say we're together
from this moment on,
or at least until
Mr. Right comes along.
It's not really cheating
as far as you see.
You're just interviewing
the next Mr. me.*

*You had another
when you first met me.
You said it was over
and that you were free.
Now I have to wonder
as we reach the end.
Were you telling him
that I was your friend?*

*I saw the hurt
and the look of surprise.
He had been fooled
by all your lies.
Now that it's my turn,
I see that it's true.
You're wanting your cake
and eating it too.*

*I won't stand around
while you play your game.
Today or tomorrow,
the ending's the same.
If this is the way
it's going to be.
You can look all you want,
just not with me.*

Relationships

*Relationships either work out
or they play out.*

I Yearn

I yearn to gaze into you eyes,
the window of your soul,
and see that you agree with me,
we make each other whole.
I yearn to know your deepest thoughts
and everything that's you.
To share my body and my soul
in everything we do.

I yearn to take you in my arms
and draw your lips to mine.
To taste the essence of your kiss
as our two hearts entwine.
I yearn for your surrender
as you give your love so free.
And know that from this moment on
there'll be no one but me.

I yearn to know that you'll be here
with hungry heart aflame,
and ache to share our passion,
knowing that I feel the same.
I yearn to take you to that place
where only lovers go,
and hear you say "I love you"
even though you know I know.

I yearn to wake each day with you
the first thing that I see,
and know that it will be this way
throughout eternity.
I yearn to know that you'll be here
to help me on my way,
and that I'll take my final breath
in loving arms one day.

I'll Crawl Through Glass

We had a fight that awful night
and you walked out on me.
You said you had to have your way
and that's how it would be.
I thought that I was in the right.
In time you'd see it too.
But now that you're away,
I find that I agree with you.

I can't hold out much longer.
You've got the best of me.
The more I think about your side,
the more that I agree.
Forget the fight, you know you're right.
Let's end this misery.
I'll crawl through glass to kiss your ass,
if you'll come back to me.

"My way or the highway"
were the last words that you said.
If that's the way that I must live,
I'd just as soon be dead.
But I have kept on living
and I have come to see.
There are some things that are much worse
than have you bossing me.

So here I stand with hat in hand
then down on bended knee.
I'll be your slave and I'll behave
if you'll come back to me.
Every home must have a head
and it must have a rear.
I'll have the last word every time
and it will be "Yes dear."

It's Not Called Cheatin' Anymore

Now that I am your "used to be".
It doesn't really matter who you see.
We both know what you're longing for.
It's not called cheatin' anymore.

It's not called cheatin' anymore.
You're still doing what you did before.
Since the day that I walked out the door.
It's not called cheatin' anymore.

I tried so hard to keep you true to me.
But when I'd look into you eyes I'd see.
That new and different is what you adore.
It's not called cheatin' anymore.

It's not called cheatin' anymore.
You're free to look for what
you're longing for.
You've taken all I have.
There's nothing more.
It's not called cheatin' anymore.

There are some people
that no one can change.
They're always looking 'round
for someone strange.
True love with only one is just a bore.
It's not called cheatin' anymore.

Two Friends

*We each need two friends.
Of this, there's no doubt.*

*One lands us in jail,
and one bails us out.*

Haikus

Seasonal Artistry

*Each season unfolds,
showing nature's artistry.
Inimitable.*

Spring

*Spring awakens Earth,
opening buds to the sun.
Many shades of green.*

Summer

*With summer's fullness,
nature's splendor is revealed,
the spectrum exposed.*

Autumn

*Colors of Autumn,
indicate maturity.
Reap what you have sown.*

Winter

*Winter's black and white,
with crisp day and frosty night.
Earth and man find rest.*

Keep It Simple Sir (K.I.S.S.)

Keep it simple sir, I say.
You're not impressing me.
Words don't make your subject more
than It was meant to be.

Does it change the meaning,
or soften the intent?
If what you're thinking's round and fat.
but you say corpulent?

The air around you smells the same,
whether gas or flatulence?
And lust is still a deadly sin
though masked as concupiscence.

Some times I wonder where you're from.
Where words are used that twist the tongue.
It doesn't help me all that much,
when you say you're indigenous.

We've reached that special time of year
for making promises so lame.
So tell me how your health's improved
by sitting, watching that bowl game?

Now's the time for a solution.
Make a New Year's resolution.
Stick with words used every day,
and spend your time on what you say.

Just Me

One week without you
is a new leather coat.
In a couple of months,
I can buy a bass boat.
I don't know now
why I took it so bad.
When you were mine,
you were all that I had.

When we were together,
your love was such,
I didn't know
I was missing so much.
But now that you're gone,
I've had time to see.
There's much more to life,
now it's all about me.

I didn't think much
of material things.
I had the contentment
that only love brings.
Now without all
of your bills to pay.
I find myself shopping
almost every day.

When we were a couple,
it was all about you.
Keeping you happy
took all I could do.
Now it's so different,
for I finally see.
It's much easier trying
to satisfy me.

*I still like the ladies
and given the chance.
I'll take one to dinner,
then maybe to dance.
But I'll be more careful
which women I choose.
Now that I know
how much I have to lose.*

Limerick of a Hooker

The lady was quite a looker.
She asked a date, so he took her.
Much later she said,
as they went to bed,
"two hundred bucks, I'm a hooker"

Maturity

*Allow your mind to mature,
but keep your heart forever young.*

Lillie

*I was headed up north
for another load.
It was just breaking dawn,
and I owned the road.
A good night's sleep,
I was feeling good.
Taking the curves
as fast as I could.*

*County lines clicked by
at a fairly good pace.
I was Mario Andretti
in a one man race.
A casual glance
in my rear view,
revealed black and white,
with flashing blue.*

*I pulled to the side
preparing my fight.
He'd accuse me of speeding.
I knew he was right.
A bear of a man
with a friendly smile.
He might let me go!
I thought for awhile.*

*He asked for my papers
and went to the rear.
He's running my license.
I've nothing to fear.
I hadn't been stopped
in almost a year.
I'd paid all my fines.
My record was clear.*

*When he came around
he was toting' his book.
His smile was replaced
by a different look.
He said you were speeding,
now you have to pay.
He gave me a ticket.
Said "have a safe day".*

*If you're ever down south
near a sleepy old town,
And it's name is Lillie,
you'd better slow down.
All towns have expenses
that someone must pay.
If you speed through Lillie,
it will ruin your day.*

Success

*If you cannot fail,
neither can you succeed*

Lover's Place

*There is a place,
somewhere in space,
reserved for lovers only.
When you are there,
you're free from care,
and no one's ever lonely.*

*There's only fear
to hold you here
when love comes on the scene.
Just let it go
and soon you'll know
exactly what I mean.*

*The ride is free,
or seems to be,
and yet you'll give your all.
Your hopes you'll pack,
hold nothing back,
when true love comes to call.*

*On passion's ride,
with love as guide,
you'll leave this world behind.
Your soul you'll bare,
and your dreams share,
and you'll be of one mind.*

*You'll soar above,
on wings of love,
as your two hearts embrace.
And then you'll know
where lovers go.
You'll find there is a place.*

Luck

I used to be a winner.
I'd seldom ever lose.
One ticket or a dozen,
mine was the one they'd choose.

Now all that's changed,
I don't complain,
I take it all in stride.
I know the only winner then
was just my foolish pride.

Let others think they're lucky,
I believe they're wrong.
I didn't know what true luck was
until you came along.

I am content
with money spent,
it goes to charity.
Soon they'll call a number
and I know it won't be me.

Now I watch as they pass by,
the winning stub in hand.
They smile as if they think
they're part of a grander plan.

The smile I give is genuine,
there is no jealousy.
They can have their winnings
and I'll keep who's here with me.

I'll never win the Lottery
and bingo's not my game.
Every time I play, I lose.
It always ends the same.

But don't think I'm a loser,
the opposite is true.
I just used up all my luck
when I met you.

Memory

*It wasn't me who caused you pain,
I wasn't even there.
The only crime I'm guilty of
is showing you I care.
Yet every time I pull you near,
I run into a wall,
and I can tell it's times like these,
his memory comes to call.*

*I'm paying for the things
he did to you.
I can't escape his memory,
no matter what I do.
The clouds of doubt come rolling in.
I know what lies in store.
I'll have to pay the price
that comes with loving you once more.*

*You tell me you want true love.
The kind you know will last.
But we can't build a future,
while clinging to the past.
I'll give you all the love I have
until my dying day.
But every time I try,
I find his memory in the way.*

*A look of love comes to your eyes,
that's just as quickly gone.
But it's that glimpse of what could be,
that keeps me hanging on.
I have to hope that someday,
time will help to ease the pain.
And you will open up your heart
and let it love again.*

Love

*Love is enjoying things
you don't really like*

Micro-Management

*It is a shame this cannot be
the way they show it on TV.
That cheer you do!
Who's kidding who?
You don't have to sell it,
if it's really true.*

*You must be the smart one.
You have a degree.
But that kind of knowledge
does not impress me.
You act so important, but little I care,
until you're as old as my underwear.*

*You schedule me forty
not one minute more.
But the work you assign will take forty four.
Then you try to push me.
You don't seem to know.
The more you're around, the slower I go.*

*You pay me to walk
but expect me to run.
You leave all those notes
of things to be done.
I really enjoy the work that I do,
and part of the fun is messing with you.*

*Do you really know how hourly folks feel?
Perhaps I can help you discern what is real.
I think our new motto
tells just how we're prone:
"Don't sweat on their time,
nor pee on your own."*

*You act like you know
how long each task takes.
But do you allow for
covering up your mistakes?
I think you should know before you begin.
Don't start up with me,
'cause you will not win.*

Teachers

*For most of us, when we think fall,
it's rake the leaves or watch football.*

*But for a teacher, it's much more.
It's back to school, young minds to bore.*

*We envy them at end of spring.
We think they're on vacation.*

*But we don't know how difficult,
their continued education.*

Mother

*The first thing that I knew of life,
through tears of joy and pain,
was Mother's adoration and
the sound of love's refrain.
She guided me, and without fail,
helped me to find my place.
How is it one so small and frail
leaves such an empty space?*

*I've never known a time without
her caring loving ways.
Now I have only memories
to fill these lonely days.
She was my mother and my friend,
my closest confidant.
She gladly gave her very best,
that I might never want.*

*I know God has a plan for us,
not understood by man.
Now I must go on without her,
though I'm not sure I can.
She led me here and showed me how
to live and love and more.
I know that she'll be waiting there,
to lead through Heaven's door.*

My Name is Shelia

*Today is the day
I take charge of my life.
I'll live it no longer
as your battered wife.
I've given you love
for these twenty years,
while you recompensed me
with bruises and tears.*

*You do not deserve love,
'cause you've none to give,
so you must release me,
it's my turn to live.
I stayed for the children,
but now they are grown.
I can think of my needs,
they're now on their own.*

*I wish you the best,
yet it cannot come true,
until you take charge
of the things that you do.
It isn't my fault
that you get so mad.
There's evil inside you
that you've always had.*

*I thought that my love
could wipe out your past.
Now I'm face to face
with the cold truth at last.
There's no more to give,
experience has shown.
I tried hard to help you,
but I worked alone.*

*I've had many names
while I've been with you.
There's bitch, skank and slut,
to mention a few.
I'm not your servant,
your slave, nor your whore.
I will answer to none
of those names anymore.*

*I was given a name
on the day of my birth.
It's what I'll respond to
for my time on earth.
They all call me Shelia
and for now so will you.
You don't have to like it,
but it's what you will do.*

*I'm not really angry.
I feel nothing at all.
The years that you hurt me
have built up a wall.
You thought I was helpless,
that I had to stay,
but now you know different,
starting today.*

*It's time to divide
what we used to share.
Now it's up to a judge
to say what goes where.
I'll take my pride
and leave you the shame.
I've already told them,
I'll take back my name.*

Miss Behavin'

*They call her Miss Behavin'.
She's a lady, that's for sure.
She is so prim and proper,
every thought and action pure.
Her eyes are soft and gentle,
and her Mona Lisa smile,
shows the world a lady
of true elegance and style.*

*But sometimes when it's late at night,
and she's alone with me,
a change comes over her
that no one else will ever see.
Her eyes now show a different glow
that springs from passion's well.
Her lips speak of an ecstasy
that only time will tell.*

*The lady who came in with me,
and quietly locked the door,
shed her inhibitions
like the clothing on the floor.
Her Mona Lisa smile is now
a sweet but impish grin,
and little Miss Behavin's
misbehavin' once again.*

Season of Confusion

*There was a time I can recall,
with just one season in the fall.
A time to carefully turn the soil,
and harvest food from Summer's toil.
We'd pick the best from God's utopia
for pantry, jars and cornucopia.*

*Then we'd invite our loved ones in
to spend some time with kith and kin.
We'd watch the table being spread,
and know we'd soon be overfed.
When all the men were filled with stuffing,
we'd pull their fingers. They weren't bluffing.*

*Now greedy merchants cannot wait,
and in their haste to decorate,
it's getting hard for me to say
what is this season's holiday.
The lines between are getting murky.
There's witches, Santa Claus and turkey.*

Vandalism

Gossip, is character vandalism.

Old Dancer

I was out for the evening
on a country dance floor,
when an elderly man
came through the front door.
He was bent nearly double,
and walked with great care.
For a moment I wondered
why he would be there.

He paid to get in
and found him a chair.
He gazed so intently,
it was almost a stare.
He watched all the dancers,
enjoying the show.
But why was he smiling?
I just had to know.

When the band took a break,
I asked to sit down.
He pushed out a chair.
I ordered a round.
We talked for a moment
of weather and such.
Then I asked the question
that vexed me so much.

He said "you remind me
of a happier time.
When I was your age
and still in my prime.
There wasn't a dance step
I couldn't do,
and people would watch me
like I'm watching you.

*When I see you dancing
and a country band plays,
for a while, I go back there
to my younger days.
I treated the ladies
with respect like you show.
If I asked for a dance,
no one ever said no.*

*You just see an old man.
There's no way to know.
I still have the memories
of times long ago.
I lived to the fullest
each day as it came.
When I went to dances,
they knew me by name.*

*You spoke of regrets.
I may have a few.
No more and no less
than other folks do.
I wish I had someone
to share my last days.
Now I'm old and feeble
and set in my ways.*

*Would I change a thing,
If given the chance?
I'd spend time with family,
friends and romance.
There once was a time
I had all this to hold.
Now nobody wants me;
bent, gray and old.*

*Enjoy the moment,
but listen to me.
There's much more to life
than what you now see.
Find someone to love you
and don't miss your chance,
by squandering all
of your youth on the dance.*

*I'm glad you came over,
and we had this talk.
In my mind I'm dancing,
though I barely walk.
So I sit here watching
and relive for awhile.
Now you know the reason
why you see a smile".*

*The band started playing.
I went to the floor.
But it wasn't about
just the dance anymore.
I knew I'd been changed
from that moment on.
When the song ended,
the old man was gone.*

Our Love

This may be too good to be true.
I've wondered from the start.
These are the things I tell my head,
but can't convince my heart.

I find I'm caught up in your spell
and feel "me" slip away,
'til where I stop and we begin,
I really cannot say.

To those we know
we're still brand new,
or have we always been?
Although we measure time in days,
we still "remember when".

There is a lot we have to learn,
and yet we know it all.
We always talk so openly
and let the pieces fall.

We feel as though we were "back then",
but really can't remember when.
Perhaps all those who're in our past
have helped us find true love at last.

My life without you here with me
would not be worth the breath.
To think we might have never been,
still scares me half to death.

Will our love stand the test of time?
No one on earth can know.
All I can do is pray each day,
that God will help it grow.

Obesity

Want not, waist not.

Strength

*You can't know what you're made of
'til your back's against the wall,
nor scale the highest mountain,
if you're fearful of the fall.*

*You won't learn of true courage
without heeding duty's call,
nor know how much is in you,
unless you have given all.*

Cancer

*It's five AM.
She stirs in her bed.
By force of habit,
she touches her head.
To see if these things
are as bad as they seem.
It often feels more like
a terrible dream.*

*Her fears are confirmed,
as hand touches skin.
With nothing remaining
where hair once had been.
The pain in her breast
tells her she's alive.
She knows all too well
the odds she'll survive.*

*She puts on a hat,
Her baldness to mask.
Then struggles to rise
for her daily task.
With four hungry mouths,
there's meals to prepare.
The children still need her,
and she will be there.*

*Life must go on,
and she's learned the trick.
"Put on a brave smile,
knowing you're sick".
She has her family,
and she'll do her part.
The cancer inside her
has not touched her heart.*

Eighty Years

*So what is it like
to experience four score?
To see the advent of autos,
airplanes and more.
From candle and lamp
to the electric light.
With the brightness of noon
now brought to the night.*

*The comforts of home.
Where do you begin?
The outhouse is gone.
We've brought it all in.
Those good old days
sometimes were hard.
We drew all our water
from a well in the yard.*

*What about housework?
We've come a long way.
At one time there wasn't
enough hours in a day.
Now there's a machine
for most any chore.
That frees up our time
to do so much more.*

*When it comes to cooking
you just turn a knob.
Once heating the oven
was half of the job.
You have to admit
these new days are good.
Whole house comfort
over fan and fire wood.*

*We have satellites in orbit
to keep us in touch.
Who would have thought
they could offer so much?
Over five hundred channels.
Which one do you choose?
Some show just weather
and others all news.*

*Wherever you go
you're never alone,
as long as you carry
your cellular phone.
Opinions may vary
whether blessing or curse,
to have all that contact
as close as your purse.*

*Those one lane roads
made of gravel and clay,
are concrete and asphalt,
the super highway.
The horseless carriage
at ten miles an hour,
now easily goes seventy,
with five hundred horsepower.*

*Who would have thought
from that very first flight,
we could now go to Europe
and be home by night.
There's talk we may colonize
Mars very soon.
We've already landed
two men on the moon.*

*You raised up five children
when the going was tough.
You sacrificed daily
so they'd have enough.
Each one is grateful
for all that you've done.
Now today it is your turn,
you're that special one.*

*So relax and be pampered,
you've sure earned your rest,
and know we want nothing
for you but the best.
We've come to join with you
to help celebrate,
the passing of time
and the decades of eight.*

*Juanita Bruffett
(May 26, 1924–January 18, 2005)*

Limerick of Paul

Paul went to the Lord with a plea.
"This thorn in the flesh torments me".
The answer God wrought,
was not what Paul sought.
"My grace is sufficient for thee".

Personals

*I opened up the paper,
as I do most every day,
to check a columnist or two
for what they have to say.
Some times I scan it quickly,
if I'm in that frame of mind,
or I may read more carefully
when I feel I have the time.*

*I was in a lazy mood,
with nothing much to do,
so I stopped to read the personals
to have a laugh or two.
The first were as expected.
They were looking for someone
to maybe share a movie with
and have a little fun.*

*Each was assigned a number
to guard their privacy.
It didn't seem that personal
but maybe that's just me.
A lady workaholic wrote of
schedules that were tight.
I wonder; will it loosen up
if she finds Mr. Right?*

*Then the tone began to change
from frivolous to sad.
I read about the single mom,
the lonely, widowed dad.
As I read between the lines,
I thought that I could see.
Some were masking loneliness
and abject misery.*

*There was one in particular
that brought me back again.
She tried to sound uplifting,
yet somehow I felt her pain.
All her interest could be shared,
or could be done alone.
I felt as if I knew her
before I picked up the phone.*

Labor of love

*A ritual occurs
three time each day,
for grownups at work,
or children at play.
They stop what they're doing.
It's time to come in,
and enjoy your labor
of love once again.*

Retired

*Everything's changed,
now that you've retired.
You can eat when you're hungry
and rest when you're tired.*

*There's no alarm clock
like those working guys.
If you're up before dawn,
it's to watch the sun rise.*

*There's no daily schedule
that you have to meet.
No long list of tasks,
you have to complete*

*There's no surly boss
to stand over you.
And take all the credit
for the work that you do.*

*There's social security
to help pay a bill,
and Medicare,
should you become ill.*

*You could go on working,
but you ask yourself. "Why"?
You'll be taken care of
'til the day that you die.*

*These are the stories
you've always been told,
to help you accept
that you're growing old.*

*The simple truth is
that when you're retired,
you'll enjoy it more,
but work twice as hard.*

*There isn't a clock,
to account for your time.
You'll work dawn to dusk,
and not earn a dime.*

Phone message

It's just a machine.
There's no need to freak.
Wait for the tone,
then you can speak.
When you've said all
that you have to say,
hang up the phone,
and have a nice day.

Journey

*It's not the steps that tire you out.
It's the stops and starts.*

Roses   (1st version)

*I planted roses in the fall
with dreams of lovely flowers.
I carefully weeded, pruned and sprayed.
I worked for hours and hours.
When with the spring no blossoms came
to show for all my toil,
I did what all good gardeners do,
and blamed it on the soil.*

*Then I met you and with a kiss
and spoken words of love,
my roses bloomed with beauty
surely sent from up above.
I watched in awe as each spring thaw
brought beauty forth with it.
I tried to copy what you did.
It didn't help a bit.*

*It wasn't til we parted ways
that I began to see,
how you could make my roses grow,
and why they just mocked me.
It wasn't that your lips were sweet,
your accent from the south.
My roses liked you best because
you have a potty mouth.*

Roses   *(2nd version)*

*I planted roses in the fall
with dreams of lovely flowers.
I carefully weeded, pruned and sprayed.
I worked for hours and hours.*

*When with the spring no blossoms came
to show for all my toil,
I did what all good gardeners do,
and blamed it on the soil.*

*Then I met you and with a kiss
and spoken words of love,
my roses bloomed with beauty
surely sent from up above.*

*I watched in awe as each spring thaw
brought beauty forth with it.
I tried to copy what you did.
It didn't help a bit.*

*We'd sit for hours among the flowers
and talk while holding hands.
I opened up my heart and spoke
of dreams and hopes and plans.*

*Then one day you went away
and left me with a note.
I went into the garden
to read the things you wrote.*

*Each line confirmed my deepest fears.
When I had read it all,
I saw our roses through my tears
and watched the petals fall.*

Respect

*Great men command respect,
small men demand it.*

Vows

*I knew when I saw you
that very first time.
I'd never be happy,
until you were mine.
So I'm here before you
on my bended knee,
promising forever
all there is of me.*

*I offer this token
to go with my heart.
We both know you've had it,
no doubt from the start.
The diamond's eternal,
the same as my love.
I avow it to you
and to Heaven above.*

She wants what you have

The key to happiness
is just as simple as it's true.
You don't get it from others,
it all begins with you.
The more you try to give away,
the more you'll have to share.
But if you take more that you give,
you'll find the cupboard bare.

The love you give so readily's
reflected back to you.
It's really easy loving one
whose heart you know is true.
So even if she had your man,
it wouldn't be the same.
She'd only take and never give
and play her cheatin' game.

There is no need to worry,
she can never get to me.
I know she wants your happiness,
but it can never be.
It isn't me that swells your heart
and sets your face aglow.
It's something deep inside of you
that she will never know.

She only takes and never gives
and still she can't explain,
why she is never happy
and each new love ends in pain.
If she would open up her heart
and give her love away,
then you can bet that what we have
would come to her one day.

Dancer   *(1st version)*

*She is an artist
in her own right.
And creates such beauty
when she's out at night.
It isn't like anything
you've seen before.
She'll paint you a picture
out on the dance floor.*

*The rhythm holds her
as if in a trance.
This lady whose heart
is attuned to the dance.
She spins and she twirls,
her story to tell.
And those who are watching
are caught in her spell.*

*The tools of her trade
didn't come from a store.
Her body's the brush
and her canvas the floor.
Her paint is the music
we've all heard before.
When she dances to it,
it means so much more.*

*So watch and admire her,
the rest of us do.
You'll feel like she's painting
that picture for you.
But her heart is free
and without a care.
She doesn't know
that you're even there.*

She'll dance with others
yet she paints alone.
She will be single
when it's time to go home.
Don't try to win her,
you haven't a chance.
There's room in her heart
for only the dance.

Dancer   (2nd version)

*She is an artist
in her own right,
and creates such beauty
when she's out at night.
It isn't like anything
you've seen before.
She'll paint you a picture
out on the dance floor.*

*The rhythm holds her
as if in a trance.
This lady whose heart
is attuned to the dance.
She spins and she twirls,
her story to tell.
And those who are watching
are caught in her spell.*

*The tools of her trade
didn't come from a store.
Her body's the brush
and her canvas the floor.
Her paint is the music
we've all heard before.
When she dances to it,
it means so much more.*

*So watch and admire her,
the rest of us do.
You'll feel like she's painting
that picture for you.
But her heart is free
and without a care.
She doesn't know
that you're even there.*

*There's room in her heart
for more than the dance,
but the lady won't settle
for casual romance.
If you're someone special
whose heart can be true,
she might share her canvas
and paint brush with you.*

*I'll do what I can.
On my butt, you'll find enough skin.*

*The surgery gave back his smile.
Everyone liked his new style.
And there by his side,
stood his blushing bride.
She couldn't sit down for awhile.*

*They went out for some wine and food.
He was in a sensitive mood.
He said to his wife
"You gave me new life.
How can I show my gratitude"?*

*She looked at his new face so sleek
and said in a voice soft and meek.
"There's naught to repay.
I get mine each day,
when your mother kisses your cheek".*

The Country Singer

*Is your voice any sweeter
than down here below?
When you sing for Jesus,
do you steal the show?
With a host of Heaven's angels
to sing harmony,
I cannot imagine
what a sound that must be.*

*You were with us a moment,
and for that we give praise.
Man was never intended
to measure his days.
The gift you brought with you,
we cherish each day.
We keep you here with us
through songs that we play.*

*To know you and love you
was one and the same.
Some eyes still glaze over
when they speak your name.
A sweet, lonely memory
is something we share.
It gives us great comfort
that you're singing there.*

*Some day we'll cross over
to see you again.
We'll hold to your memory
and wait until then.
What a time that will be
in the sweet by and by.
When we join you forever
to sing in the sky.*

Roger Lee Werle
(October 14, 1937–May 17, 2001)

Sick

*You say that you're sick
and now I've got it too.
It doesn't feel anything
close to the flu.
I'm tired and I'm grouchy
and I'm achy too.
You're sick of me
and now I'm sick of you.*

*You told me that you
had a touch of the flu,
and we couldn't do
what we planned to do.
So I drove by your house
around closing time.
The car in your driveway
sure wasn't mine.*

*I saw the shadow
of you on the blind.
A man held you tightly
and you didn't mind.
I don't know of anything
that I can do.
I'm glad you feel better
and wish I did too.*

*How I made it home
I won't ever know.
It must be that my car
knows how it should go.
I tossed and I turned
thinking what I could do.
I hope your new man
comes down with the flu.*

Space

I stare at the closet,
where her clothes used to be.
She carried out the threat
to not live with me.

It didn't seem serious.
She had said it before.
But things would settle down
before she reached the door.

This time it was dif'rent,
for there were no tears.
She'd finally given up.
This space holds my fears.

Now I would like to talk,
but there's no one to hear.
I would even listen,
To show how much I care.

Take this advice I'm offering,
before it's too late for you.
Spend a little time each day,
or you'll end up here too.

The chance I had to make things right
Is just a memory.
She didn't have to leave.
The blame belongs to me.

I can refill the closet
where her clothes used to be,
but how will I fill
the space inside me?

Not easy

If it was easy, anyone could do it.

Summer wind

Who's to say what really matters,
when it comes to loving you.
Is the love that lasts forever,
the only one that's really true.
If the time we spent together
was the best that's ever been,
maybe love is like a snowflake,
drifting on a summer wind.

I knew the night I met you
that you weren't the one for me.
There was something strong between us,
but it wasn't meant to be.
We tried to build a future
on our love and nothing more.
Now it's ending as it has to
with me walking out your door.

There isn't anyone to blame
for things that we have done.
We are just two different people
and we never can be one.
Now we're standing at the threshold,
knowing what we have to do.
And it hurts so much to leave here
'cause I'm still in love with you.

Maybe soon you'll meet the person
that you wanted me to be.
You deserve a special someone
and I wish it could be me.
We could blame it on each other,
but we know that isn't true.
Some are meant to love forever,
others just a year or two.

Retirement Community

*The voice on the phone
was inviting enough.
But what's the real story
behind all the fluff?
I know of these places
with all of their ills.
Where old folks sit staring
awaiting their pills.*

*It's your decision.
It's not up to me.
But I'll go with you.
How bad can it be?
I have an opinion
of how these places are.
I'll keep my mind open
on the way in the car.*

*The grounds are well kept
and as neat as a pin.
It's all very pretty.
I hate to go in.
I'm sure it will change
once we get inside.
There's only so much,
paint and paper can hide.*

*The entry is spacious,
so open and light.
Not at all as expected.
There's something not right.
The people are elderly,
at least that part is true.
They're visiting and laughing.
They're friendly too.*

*Here is the person
who helps run the place.
The voice on the phone
now has a kind face.
Would I like a tour?
I believe that I would.
I'm starting to think
this could do you some good.

There are people who clean
your apartment for you.
They change out your linens
and do laundry too.
Your meals are prepared
with nutrition foremost.
You need only relax
while served by your host.

Everything's furnished
except for the phone.
With all these great people,
you need not be alone.
I have one last question,
and it concerns me.
Before I can move in,
how old must I be?*

Yard Sale

A painted sign read "Yard Sale",
so I pulled my old car in.
I come across a bargain
every now and then.
You never know what treasures
you might find buried there,
that really don't need much at all,
just tender loving care.

The sale was sort of trashy,
as many of them are.
I took a final look around
as I went to my car.
When there among the rubble,
I somehow chanced to see
something which took my breath
away from me.

A small and fragile figurine,
which seemed so out of place.
The wings were made of crystal,
with porcelain for it's face.
The price marked there upon the tag,
did not reflect the worth
of the sweetest memories
of our shared time on earth.

I picked it up so tenderly
and drew it close to me.
Then turned away from others,
so no one there would see.
Remembering you once held it
when I gave it to you.
You promised that forever
your love for me was true.

I saw a lonely looking man,
whose face was drawn and pale.
I knew without a doubt
this had to be his sale.
I felt as though I'd met him,
but I could not recall.
He had a most familiar look
about him after all.

I paid him for my mem'ry,
with feelings barely masked.
I took a slow and careful breath,
before I quietly asked.
How was it he had owned this piece
which seemed to me so nice?
Why was it he would sell it
for a paltry yard sale price?

I saw that sad look on his face
I'd come to recognize.
His lips began to quiver
and tears came to his eyes.
I knew without him saying,
I was standing face to face
with the broken hearted man
you has used to take my place.

I wanted so to hate him,
but it would just be wrong.
He didn't know that you were mine
until he came along.
Perhaps somehow I'd help him,
but what was I to do.
It might make him feel better
if I talked to him of you.

*It's not his fault that you are gone,
no more than it was mine.
You just get restless for a change
and leave from time to time.
I may find strength to talk to him,
but it won't be today.
I wrote his address in my book,
then quickly drove away.*

Tomatoes

*The only time I know for sure
that what I'm doing's right,
is when I pick tomatoes
in the early morning light.
They're either ready or they're not.
There is no in between.
The color of their flesh reveals
if they are ripe or green.*

*They never tease, they always please,
they're pretty much the same.
You know exactly how they'll be,
there isn't any game.
They give you everything they have
and do not ask for much.
A little nurturing each day.
A tender, caring touch.*

*So how is it I find myself
here listening to this band.
To catch a special lady's eye
and take her by the hand.
A pretty face, a close embrace,
a slow romantic song.
If what we're doing isn't right,
I'd just as soon be wrong.*

*Tomorrow morning I'll return
to what makes my heart stir.
My hands will pick tomatoes
while my thoughts will be of her.
I'll carefully select the best
that nature holds in store,
and wait until I have the chance
to hold her close once more.*

The Voice

There is a voice that haunts my dreams
and every waking hour.
How can a sound that is so soft
hold such an awesome power?
We've never met, and even yet,
there's no one else for me.
I shun them all, await her call,
and live on imagery.

She never meant to place the call,
her fingers slipped a bit.
She tried to end, not to offend,
and yet we didn't quit.
She revealed her inner thoughts,
as three hours turned to four.
I told her things I've never said
to anyone before.

If I could meet her face to face,
would it help to break the spell?
I don't know what the future holds,
and only time will tell.
For now, I'll wait to hear from her,
and hope she feels the same.
She didn't give a number
and told only her first name.

Will she ever call again?
Was it a one time thing?
Was there a need that's been fulfilled?
Will my phone ever ring?
These questions plague me even now
as I sit here alone.
While daylight turns to darkness,
I stare at my silent phone.

Creativity

Creativity, is viewing the ordinary, in an extraordinary way.

The Glow

*The weather outside
is cloudy and glum.
So where is the smile
on her face coming from?*

*There is a tingle
from her head to her toe.
Her heart holds the secret
of an internal glow.*

*What is the secret
she's keeping from me?
Is her life as happy
as it seems to be?*

*She's learned all the lessons
as she's moved along,
and faces the music
with her special song.*

*She has the same problems
that trouble mankind.
Yet she knows each dark cloud,
is still silver lined.*

Clean mind

To keep your mind clean, you must change it once in awhile.

The Wall

*How many have died,
with no name on the wall?
How many were killed there,
but have yet to fall?
How many young boys
came back broken men,
with a troubled void,
where their soul once had been?*

*How many died later,
without wounds that show,
with scars running deeper
than we'll ever know?
When we count the cost
of that awful war,
fifty-six thousand,
but each day adds more.*

*How many soldiers
who lived through that Hell,
still walk among us
as only a shell,
of what they once were
before they got the call?
They'll die far too young,
with no name on the wall.*

The Editor

*Who do you offend,
when you take up your pen,
to change my words into yours?*

*You offend all the ones
whose daughters and sons
have died on faraway shores.*

*You offend those who fight,
to give us the right,
to express ourselves as we do.*

*And if you're a poet,
though you may not know it,
you also offend even you.*

*So the next time you're
in an editing mood,
and decide that's the way to behave.*

*Instead take a trip
to Arlington
and spit on a soldier's grave.*

Vocabulary

Big words do not enhance small thoughts.

Santa Claus

Excuse me, Mister Santa Claus,
I really need to talk.
I'm not asking for a present,
I only want to walk.

They say I'll always be this way,
I don't believe it's true.
This is the time for miracles,
I'm asking one from you.

I only want to run and play,
the way my brothers do.
My mom and dad can't give me this,
so now it's up to you.

Each night, I pray that with the dawn,
I'll have the strength to walk.
I'm sure that it will happen now,
since we have had this talk.

I can't wait 'til Christmas day,
to see what's waiting there.
You'll find some cookies and some milk,
right next to my wheel chair.

Failure

You don't fail, until you stop trying.

The Man

I'm not the man I used to be,
and probably never was.
If it seems better now than then,
it may be just because.

Success is easy to review,
while failure pains the soul,
so over time it tends to skew,
'til part becomes the whole.

I'm not as humble as some are.
I think I'm better off by far,
to face the world with honesty,
and not with false humility.

History may not judge the same,
and cast aspersions on my name,
while I'm content with memory
of twice the man I used to be.

Limerick of Youth

There once was a time in my youth,
I might have been somewhat uncouth.
On many a night,
there'd be a fist fight,
and I, more than once, lost a tooth.

The Kiss

*Our worlds are so different,
I knew from the start.
But that's not the feeling,
that came from my heart.
My mind told me end it.
Love can't be like this.
If I could start over,
I'd take back the kiss.*

*I knew when I met you,
that we weren't the same.
I searched for true love,
while you played your game.
I must have learned something,
for now I know this.
If I could start over,
I'd take back the kiss.*

*We had things in common
that made us go on.
Then we became lovers
before very long.
Now what is so different
that makes me say this.
If I could start over,
I'd take back the kiss.*

*I don't know exactly
where we go from here.
We can't say the words
we're both longing to hear.
There are many things
that I know I will miss.
But I must start over
and take back the kiss.*

Actions

*Actions speak louder
than words so they say.
Late night time promises
may not last a day.*

*Words may be needed
to say how I feel.
But actions will tell you
that my love is real.*

*I wish I could tell you
all that's in my heart.
But words don't come easy,
I can't even start.*

*So I'll keep on doing
those things every day,
that tell you I love you
in ways I can't say.*

*I know other people
who talk easily.
They turn your head
with glib flattery.*

*But actions are different
than the things they say.
While I try to show you
my love every day.*

*I hope that in time
you'll believe as I do.
There's more than one way
to show love is true.*

*Word's may be needed
when love first begins.
It's actions that proves it
will last 'til the end.*

Angels Among Us

There are angels among us,
or so I am told.
Don't look for halos,
but hearts of pure gold.
When you call for them,
there's no place too far.
They make you feel special
'cause they know you are.

The look in their eyes
show how much they care.
They make your load lighter
by just being there.
They're some you can count on
through good times and bad.
They laugh when you're happy,
and cry when you're sad.

We each may be angels
on some special day.
When we are the ones
with just what to say
to help ease the sadness
for someone in need.
We're human by flesh,
and angels by deed.

Stand by to answer
when you hear the call.
Be ready and willing
to sacrifice all.
No greater reward
will ever be yours,
than when you are chosen
for one of God's chores.

*Whether the glass is half empty, or half full
depends upon whether you are drinking or pouring.
The same can be said of your heart.*

Artist's Eye

*I know you're a woman,
made of flesh and bone.
But you've given something
I've never known.
This is the reason
I think you're a saint.
Your heart is the palette
and love is the paint.*

*With the eye of an artist
and heart of a saint,
You work your magic
with palette and paint.
Things old and broken
are better than new.
Is it any wonder
that I worship you.*

*There are angels among us,
I've heard people say.
But I'd never met one
'til you came my way.
You found me in darkness,
and led me to light.
I'll never be worthy,
try as I might.*

*You must have seen something
as you passed by,
that only held promise
in your artist eye.
You went through the garbage
and found every part,
then you recycled
my broken heart.*

*You see past the surface
to what's deep inside.
So you know the feelings
I'm trying to hide.
I fear if I tell you,
I'll scare you away.
You know that I'll love you
'til my dying day.*

Attic

*I'm cleaning the attic.
It's been long enough.
I now have the courage
to sort through your stuff.
Some goes to Goodwill
or some other place.
What once was your memory
is taking up space.*

*It still won't be easy
to discard our life.
We did that already
as husband and wife.
We made a mistake,
now we have to pay.
It's time to start over,
beginning today.*

*I'll haul off the boxes
that you left behind.
You didn't want them
and I didn't mind,
to give them a home
for a year, maybe two.
I know how it feels,
discarded by you.*

*When this day is over,
I'll start anew.
There'll be no more boxes,
no memories of you.
What once was so full,
is now empty space.
My heart and my attic
may be the same place.*

Break Up Kit

I open the package.
My hands start to shake.
The label says fragile,
I feel my heart break.
I know what's inside it,
still I have to see.
How little remains
of what we used to be.

A toothbrush, a razor,
an old ratty comb,
are all that remain
of what we called our home.
I'll put them away
and not use them again.
Except to remind me
of what might have been.

I look at the picture.
An old eight by ten.
The smiles on our faces
show how we were then.
We were so happy
when our love was new.
Now this break up package
tells me we're through.

The letters are tied
by a ribbon of red.
I loosen the bow
with a feeling of dread.
I know they hold promise,
that turned into lies.
But now I can't read them,
through tears in my eyes.

*I close up the package
and store it away.
I've had all the memories
I need for today.
Time's a great healer,
I've heard people say.
If that ever happens,
I'll throw it away.*

Chatham

*A quiet little town
outside the rat race.
With hard working folk
and old southern grace.
If you're getting tired
of your hectic pace,
our town called Chatham
just might be the place.*

*We have a sheriff,
who's always around.
We don't lock the doors
in our little town.
If mischief's about,
it keeps out of sight.
We always feel safe,
even at night.*

*There's only one barber
in our little town.
A tonsorial artist
of widespread renown.
A friendly old fellow
who could be retired.
He's open three days
and rests when he's tired.*

*It takes thirty minutes,
but that isn't bad,
for the best hair cut
that you've ever had.
With vacuum clippers,
there's never a mess.
He charges six dollars.
No more and no less.*

*The only mechanic
for miles around,
we're proud to have here
in our little town.
He'll look at your problem
and discuss what to do.
If he cannot fix it,
there's no charge to you.*

*The hardware store
at first seems so small.
They carry most things
and can order it all.
They'll show you around
like folks used to do.
With large sale or small,
they always thank you.*

*There are three filling stations,
with groceries and more.
What you might expect
in a little town store.
The clerks are all friendly
and call you by name.
They make you feel welcome
and glad that you came.*

*We've a couple of diners
and a deli or two.
Be sure to stop in,
if you're passing through.
The best cole slaw
and fried fish around.
It's easy to brag
on our little town.*

There's a bank, a post office,
and two laundromats.
There's even a car wash,
if you need more than that,
big city shopping
is not very far.
About thirty minutes
to Monroe by car.

The pace seems so frantic,
but there's peace of mind.
To know when it's over,
you can leave it behind.
Get away from the city
as the sun's going down.
To the peace and the quiet
that's our little town.

Cheat in a small town

*You're doing things
I'd rather not know,
but gossip will follow
wherever you go.
I stay away
where I think you might be,
but cheat in a small town
and someone will see.*

*Cheat in a small town
and you'll be found out.
It may take time,
but there isn't a doubt.
Someone will see you
and then it will be,
a matter of time
'til it gets back to me.*

*What is the reason
that you're cheating, dear?
Sooner or later
you know I will hear.
Are you tired of me
being your only one,
and don't have the courage
to tell me we're done?*

*If you want your freedom,
then just tell me so.
I won't really like it,
but I'll let you go.
You don't have to act
like we are the same,
and try to keep secrets,
while you play your game.*

*I'm hoping things aren't
as they seem to be.
Maybe your double
is cheating on me.
If you say it's so,
that's the way it will be.
It seems that the whole town's
been lying to me.*

Chemistry

I thought when I first saw you,
that you weren't the one for me.
Your legs were slightly crooked,
and things weren't where they should be.
But as the night grew longer
and the beer began to flow.
I noticed you had taken on a glow.

We danced to Roger Werle's band
and all the songs were slow.
You looked so very pretty
with the lights turned way down low.
I told you all the things I know
a woman wants to hear,
and then I ordered us another beer.

They closed the bar at 2 AM
and sent us on our way.
I wondered just how you would look
beneath the light of day.
We went to sleep without a light
and when the sun arose,
you found that I was putting on my clothes.

You said I was a user
and that I would have my day.
You told me you would get me
'cause you had my DNA.
I knew I was in trouble
if I didn't answer quick,
so I asked if you would be my chick.

Chem—is—try. Chem—is—try.
That's what makes your knees go weak,
with eyes too blind to see.
If you can get past all my faults
and still be wanting me.
Then what we have
is good old chemistry.

Choices

*I only have two choices
when it comes to loving you.
If I stay, I'll hurt each day,
but leaving's painful too.
The only choice I have with you
is to decide if I'm,
to take the heart ache all at once
or a little at a time.*

*There've been a lot of choices
that I have had to make.
Either way I choose this time,
I know my heart will ache.
I must decide which way to deal
with all the hurt inside.
Shall I take it all at once
or a little at a time.*

*Knowing you, has caused me pain
I've never known before.
No matter how I try
I always leave you wanting more.
I know no man can satisfy
the hunger that you feel.
Each day there's a new wound
that only time can heal.*

*It hurts to stay. It hurts to go.
So what am I to do.
It's killing me inside to know
that I'm not pleasing you.
Perhaps it's best to end it now
and let the healing start.
If I can kick the habit,
I can mend my broken heart.*

Chosen Memories

*These chosen memories
hold me just like a chain.
All those special moments
won't let me love again.
I've forgotten the bad things
that drove us apart.
But these chosen memories
are locked in my heart.*

*You can take all the things
we shared for some time.
Put me on the street,
without even a dime.
You can turn all our friends
and keep them from me.
But the one thing you can't take
are these chosen memories.*

*I forgot all the bad times
we had near the end.
We lost the feeling
and couldn't be friends.
Now there's only ashes
where fire used to be.
All those warm embraces
are chosen memories.*

*I know all the reasons
why you left me.
I'll try to make changes,
then we will see,
if we can rekindle
what we used to be.
Then we'll be together
with chosen memories.*

Date in a Small Town

*Date in a small town
and everyone knows.
The proof's in your eyes
and the way your face glows.*

*We give you our blessing.
We're happy for you.
It tells us that there may be
hope for us too.*

*Did you really think
you could fool us for long?
You smile when you're dancing
and it's not the song.*

*That gleam in your eye
and that grin on your face,
can only mean someone's
in your special place.*

*You thought you could date
and not be found out.
Your friends know you better
and we have no doubt.*

*You're seeing someone
who's special to you.
But keep it a secret!
Just who's fooling who?*

*For now we're content
to feel love through you,
and wait for the day
we find happiness too.*

*It's good to know
there may be romance.
Until then, please save us
a song and a dance.*

Consumed

*I have consumed. I've been consumed.
I've felt love's passion rage,
and so I know the sweetest love
is one that comes with age.*

*It is expected in our youth,
for love to take us slave,
but few will race the setting sun,
while surfing passion's wave.*

*It seems as though a miracle
that this has come to be.
All I know is I thank God
for sending you to me.*

Dawn

*Come to my garden
before break of day.
Prepared to be awed
by nature's display.
Lend ear to the wind,
the bee and the bird.
The sweetest refrain
that you've ever heard.*

*Watch the sky changing
from raven to pink,
with naught to distract
as you sit and think.
Contemplate blessings
to have and to hold.
As the sun rises,
the pink turns to gold.*

*Flowers that are such
a familiar sight,
take on a new look
in pale morning light.
The shadows are long,
the air crisp and cool.
Imagine his throne,
if Earth's his footstool.*

*There's more to be seen,
God's work isn't done.
Dew's sparkling diamonds,
when kissed by the sun.
This show was produced
for no one but you.
Applaud it's creator.
Watch it turn blue.*

Doris

The sweetest smile.
The kindest eyes.
A heart much bigger
than her small size.

So quick to laugh
when others joke.
The careful thought,
before she spoke.

A loving soul
with gentle ways.
She'll be in our thoughts
the rest of our days.

Doris H. Hadfield
(September 2, 1913–March 8, 2005)

Promises

In our time of grief and doubt,
God's promises are true.

He never said he pull us out,
he said he'd pull us through.

Each day's better than the next

*Each day's better than the next.
Our love is going down hill.
We both try to fight it,
but we lack the will,
to give the things to each other,
we've both needed so long.
We don't look for others,
though the temptation's strong.*

*When we came together,
we swore love to the end.
Now what passes between us,
seems more like a friend.
You'll always be part of me,
as far as I see,
but we lack the passion,
of what used to be.*

*We had so much in common,
including our past.
We thought we'd found true love,
but it didn't last.
What brought us together,
may tear us apart.
We share all we have,
except for our heart.*

*We spend time together,
maybe too much.
If we have a lifetime,
then what is the rush.
So let's start all over,
'cause I'd like to know,
if this love's forever,
or if I should go.*

Eternity

*I have learned a new meaning
for e-tern-i-ty.
It's the time that I'm spending
when you're not with me.
I once thought forever
was as far as I see.
But now a moment without you
is e-tern-i-ty.*

*When we're out together,
I can't help but see.
How you scan the floor
while dancing with me.
I know why you're looking
and it hurts so to be,
near the end of what we thought
was e-tern-i-ty.*

*We once swore that our love
would last for all time.
There was no one between us.
I was yours and you—mine.
Now I don't see that love light
when you look at me.
What I see drawing nearer
is e-tern-i-ty.*

*Some are together,
growing closer each day.
They take comfort knowing
what they have will stay.
Others want changes
and are bored easily.
They won't know the sweetness
of e-tern-i-ty.*

No "L"

There is no "L" in Christmas,
so what's it all about?
They sing as if there once had been,
and now must do without.
Is it because the wise men
hadn't been taught how to spell,
that caused the angels to appear,
and tell them there's no "L"?

There is no "L" in Christmas,
I've known it all along.
So why is it this time of year,
they have to play that song.
There is no "L" in Christmas.
I read you loud and clear.
Just in case I might forget,
you'll sing it every year.

There is no "L" in Christmas,
so why make all the fuss?
Just because a few forget,
don't tell the rest of us.
It really tests my patience
to be told how I must spell,
so sing all of those Christmas songs,
just don't tell me no "L".

Fool

What is it in your cheatin' heart
that can't be satisfied?
You'll trade a love that's open
for one you have to hide.
You'll go out with some stranger,
then come home with your lies,
but I know you've been cheatin',
I can see it in your eyes.

I'm a fool, believing,
the things you say to me.
I'm a fool for thinking
our love could ever be.
I believe forever,
and to you that's such a bore.
I'm a fool,
but I'm not your fool anymore.

It seems to be a game to see
just how far you can go,
but it's not hard to fool someone
who doesn't want to know.
I listen while you tell your tale
about the things you did.
I bite my tongue, hold back the tears,
and keep my feelings hid.

I know there's others out there
and they're not all like you.
I'll find someone to love me
with a heart that can be true.
I know exactly what I'll say
as I walk out your door.
"I'm a fool,
but I'm not your fool anymore."

Immortality

*Immortality comes
in various ways.
Memories remain
beyond your days.*

*You have your children
to carry your name.
There was celebrity,
fortune and fame.*

*How long you're remembered
is but part of the test.
We think you were special,
apart from the rest.*

*We speak with one voice,
as we gather near.
The world is much nicer
because you were here.*

*Walter D. King
(August 10, 1922–May 29, 2004)*

Friends

*When couples break up,
what happens to friends?
Sometimes they choose one,
but that all depends,
on whether you use them
or if you've resolved,
to let them stay neutral,
and not get involved.*

*We have friends in common,
who know what you do.
They see how you're acting
when I'm not with you.
They're in a bind,
'cause they like both of us,
but they know you're someone
that I shouldn't trust.*

*Sooner or later,
friendship will win,
for they know a secret
they cannot keep in.
We'll run out of small talk
and then they'll begin
to tell me you're seeing
all those other men.*

*I know they know something,
'cause their faces show,
the sympathy I'll need
as soon as I know
what they want to tell me,
but just don't know how.
Their friendship's important,
so I'll wait for now.*

*I'm betting you used them
and now you have found,
someone to cheat with
when I'm not around.
I think that our friends
are more honest than you,
and sooner or later,
they'll tell what you do.*

*I'm sure you badmouth me
whenever you're out.
But I won't do that
'cause I have no doubt,
they will determine
who's right and who's wrong,
and make the decision
with whom they belong.*

Sister

*As a mirror reflects your image,
a sister reflects your heart.*

Honky-tonk toy

*You come from the city,
where you learned your charm.
While I'm from the country
and grew up on a farm.
So you be the lady
who fills me with joy,
and I'll be your honky-tonk toy.*

*We met at a dance hall.
It happened by chance.
We were there for the music.
We both love to dance.
We had nothing in common,
except for one thing.
We had both known of love
and we both knew its sting.*

*It was slow to develop
for our minds were strong.
We both knew we couldn't
be lovers for long.
We danced at a distance
as long as we could.
Until what seemed wrong
was over shadowed by good.*

*Finally it happened,
while the music was slow.
We made our decision
about how it would go.
We'd dance for the moment,
the future was not.
We didn't think of the time
when the music would stop.*

When the band took a break,
and the dance floor was hot,
we went for some cool air
in the bar's parking lot.
We talked of the weather
and stared into space.
Then without any warning,
I was in your embrace.

And now comes the time
we have both dreaded so.
The music is over,
there is no place to go.
I can't live in your world,
nor can you in mine,
so we've had our music,
one dance at a time.

How in the world can I miss you.

How in the world can I miss you,
when I can't even get you to leave?
How can I start being lonely,
with you hanging onto my sleeve?

I've tried everything I can think of,
and still you keep hanging on.
You tell me you know that I'd miss you,
but I won't know until you are gone.

You tell me you don't really want me.
You say you'd be fine on your own.
You act like it don't really matter
if I'm away or at home.

It's time that you made a decision.
We're either a team or apart.
I'm sure that we had something one time,
but it may not have come from the heart.

You tell me I'm cold and indifferent
and don't hear a word that you say.
Tell me while you're passing judgment,
just how many games do you play?

I know that I once tried to please you,
whatever you liked was OK.
Now I don't know what your needs are,
they're different with each passing day.

If I am such a bad person,
so selfish and just out for me,
I'd think that you would be happy,
if you were totally free.

*Each time I try to arrange it
for you to be out on your own,
you act as if I have hurt you,
by leaving you home all alone.*

*I don't know why you're so angry.
I never meant you any harm.
I tried to be your weak toady
but finally it just lost its charm.*

*You're what some would call a man hater.
You haven't much use for a male.
You seem to think their two places,
are either in court or in jail.*

*You've always said we were equal.
We share everything that we make.
Why is it I get the feeling,
that I am to give while you take?*

*Now I have just one last question
as we reach the end of the line.
Just how is it you have determined
that your half is bigger than mine?*

*I'm sure that I'll find someone some day
who'll love me just as I am.
But first I will have to forget you
and how I wound up in this jam.*

*There have to be some women out there
who bless much more than they curse.
It's time that I went for the better,
I've had all I need of the worse.*

Go Vote

You left a little note today,
to remind me what to do.
What I read as just one thing,
you'd actually written two.

It isn't really all my fault,
I did the thing you wrote.
It sounded like a single task.
"Put out the trash. Go vote."

How do you know

How do you know
when love comes to and end.
When the kisses and touches
seem more like a friend.
When the gleam in her eyes
has lost it's desire,
and there's only ashes,
where once was a fire.

The kiss of a lover
and that of a friend,
might not seem that different,
except at the end.
A friend will go from you
to a life of her own,
while a lover will linger
'til you are alone.

The touch of a lover
and that of a friend,
may only be different
in the message they send.
The friend's say I like you
and I really care,
while the lover's hold promises
beyond compare.

The eyes of a lover
and those of a friend,
may both say I love you
but what they intend,
is as different as nighttime
is from the day.
For a lover won't leave you
and go on her way.

Trust

*If love is the mortar,
then trust is the stone.
You cannot build houses
with mortar alone.
It takes both of them
to make foundations strong,
and love without trust,
won't last very long.*

*I know that you love me,
there's not any doubt,
but love's not the only thing
life is about.
I need you to trust me
and respect what I do.
You must know that I feel
this way about you.*

*True love can only
take people so far.
That is the reason
we are where we are.
If we're to move forward
from where we began,
then you'll have to trust me
as much as you can.*

*I've never done one thing
to cause you to doubt
that what I am saying
is what I'm about,
but still you must question
each thing that I do.
I think it has something
to say about you.*

I loved her just in time

I loved her just in time to lose her
and now too late I see.
I'm telling you my story,
so you won't end up like me.
If I'd returned the love she gave,
I know she'd still be mine.
I took each day for granted
until I ran out of time.

I thought I wouldn't love her
if I controlled it from the start.
I'd take the love she offered me
and still protect my heart.
I'd do the things that lovers do
and hold on to my plan.
But now she's gone and left me.
I'm a broken hearted man.

I knew just what she wanted.
I could see it in her eyes.
But still I couldn't say the words.
I thought they would be lies.
Too late I find that they were real,
but it can never be.
You can't control the way you feel.
I hope that you agree.

And now my story's ending
while yours has just begun.
You have the chance that I have lost
to be her only one.
I hope you'll learn from my mistake
and not end up like me.
You'll have the chance to love her,
so be all that you can be.

I Was There

*I was there,
when we laid down at night.
I was there,
as we fought our final fight.
You say that I'm the one to blame.
I didn't really care.
I know the truth of what went wrong.
Remember, I was there.*

*I listen while you tell your tale
with such sincerity.
You speak with such conviction
that anyone could see.
I'm the one that is to blame.
You've had all you can bear.
I wouldn't know the difference,
except that I was there.*

*It takes two to start a love affair,
but only one to quit.
Usually both must share the blame,
at least a little bit.
You tell me that it's all my fault
because I didn't care.
But if I didn't love you,
why was I always there?*

*If it makes you happy,
you can blame it all on me.
But I'm the one whose love is true
and yours don't seem to be.
I know I'm not your only one,
dispute it if you dare.
You have found another love.
I know 'cause I was there.*

Velvet Chain

*Somehow I know
before I open the door,
she'll be standing there
like always before.
The smile on her face
as I saw it last.
With no sign at all
of the months that have past.*

*She is a free spirit
and without remorse.
She asks to come in,
and I say "of course".
She enters my arms
as she was back then,
and I feel my heart
captured again.*

*She tries to convince me
she has come back.
But with only one suitcase,
she doesn't unpack,
I have to believe,
though I pray that I'm wrong,
she'll be just a memory
before very long.*

*It's not as one sided
as it seems to be.
When we're alone,
there's no one but me.
But it's always there
in the back of my mind,
when she says she loves me,
is she just being kind?*

*What is this hold
she has over me?
Each time she leaves,
I swear I'll break free.
But when she returns
it's worth all the pain,
for there's nothing stronger
than this velvet chain.*

Masquerade

*There're at least three persons
In each of us.
Who we are; who you see;
who we will be.*

*There is a person
we keep tightly furled,
that's never shown
to the rest of the world.*

*There is a person
known only to us,
with inner secrets
we never discuss.*

*How much of yourself
have you shown to me?
How much is a secret,
that I'll never see?*

*Who is the real person
behind the mask?
Would you take it off
if I were to ask?*

*You can fool others,
but what about you?
If you lie enough,
will you think it's true?*

I wish upon our star

I miss you most of all,
while I'm holding you near.
That's when I'm with a stranger,
not the love that was so dear.
You have changed into another
and I don't know who you are.
So I'll have to dream about you,
while I wish upon our star.

Once we were so happy,
we had our dreams and plan.
Now it doesn't seem to matter,
since you met another man.
I'm not accusing you of cheating,
but as far as I can see,
He's the one whose in your thoughts,
while lying here with me.

We don't talk about the future.
We live from day to day.
I try to talk about it.
You just turn and walk away.
So I guess I must accept it,
it's the way that it will be.
You must know that I still love you
and this is killing me.

Maybe someday we'll recover
all the love that we once had.
Then today can be forgotten
and in time not seem so bad.
Until then I'll hold my head up
and go on the way we are.
At least I have the memories
and can wish upon our star.

I'll wait

You don't have to tell me
how you really feel.
One look in your eyes
shows your love is real.
The way that you hold me
when the music is slow,
tells me everything
I need to know.

I know you're a lady
in the old fashioned way.
You're very careful
about what you say.
But I feel your love
growing strong with each date.
So for this moment,
I'm contented to wait.

You say it's too perfect
to ever be true.
You don't really know me
and I don't know you.
We must go slowly,
this isn't a game.
But I know I loved you
before I knew your name.

Our love is forever,
so what is the haste.
These precious moments
we mustn't waste.
So I'll take your loving
one kiss at a time.
And wait for the day
when you'll say you're mine.

Wake Up At Six

*Our very first memories
of the pleasures of life,
before we knew schedules,
or turmoil, or strife.
All snuggled in blankets
clear up to our chin.
We'd wake up at six
and get up at ten.*

*We started to school
and everything changed.
We got up so early,
each minute arranged.
We patiently waited
for the long week to end,
to wake up at six
and get up at ten.*

*When we first got married,
we barely got by.
Yet love came so easy,
we did not have to try.
We hardly could wait
for the day to begin.
'cause we'd wake up at six
and get up at ten.*

*Then came the children
and our time was gone.
Each minute was filled
from the first light of dawn.
We'd fall into bed,
our energy drained,
and pray for the strength
to repeat it again.*

*We took a vacation
away from it all.
There were no appointments,
yet we left a call,
so we could recapture
what we had back then,
when we'd wake up at six
and get up at ten.*

*Some day they'll be grown
and out on their own,
and our golden years will begin.
When we have the house
to ourselves once again,
we'll wake up at six
and get up at ten.*

I'm glad that I miss you

I'm glad that I miss you
'cause there's no other way.
To keep alive the memories
we shared 'til today.
We can't be together,
so we'll live apart.
I'll keep the memories
to help heal my heart.

We dreamed of the same things
when our love began.
Now you're wanting more
than you'll find in one man.
I may not be perfect,
though I try to be.
I know you're comparing
all others to me.

I may have some vices
like most of us do.
But you can be certain
that my love is true.
If I were to change now,
I wouldn't be me.
So I'll grant your last wish
and you can be free.

When you've had time
to be on your own.
You might find you miss me
and pick up the phone.
But if you find true love,
then that's all right too.
For I don't believe
I will always miss you.

It Didn't Kill Me

*It didn't kill me
when you walked out on me.
Least not the part
most other people see.
I've never known a thing
to hurt so bad.
It didn't kill me,
but at times I wish it had.*

*When we were one,
I gave my life to you.
You promised ever after
and a heart that would be true.
All that changed
in the blinking of an eye.
You left me broken
and alone to die.*

*When you first left,
I thought my world would end.
It hurt so deep,
my heart could never mend.
Now I know for sure
I will survive.
It's not living,
but at least I'm still alive.*

*With life there's hope,
so I'll just have to pray.
I'll find a way to heal
my heart some day.
'Til then I'll do
the things I have to do.
To ease the pain
I feel from losing you.*

Locker

*My heart's in a locker
with most of my clothes.
I didn't mark the boxes,
so only heaven knows
if I'll ever find it
and use it once again.
So I'll sit here drinking
for what might have been.*

*My things are in a locker
and my life's on hold.
You sent me a packing
and I wasn't told
you had another
who'd soon take my place.
My heart's in a locker
and my mind's in space.*

*You said we'd be together
for the rest of your life.
You even had visions
of being my wife.
Now everything's different
and I'm in a mess,
'cause nothing's important
but your happiness.*

*When we were a couple,
it seemed all was fine,
as long as I willingly
stayed within the line.
I did what you told me
and tried to keep peace.
Now our love is over,
my name's off the lease.*

Looks

*The look can show things
without words being said.
It says you're in heaven
or simply you're dead.
The look comes with faces
to go with the scene.
If you've ever had it,
you know what I mean.*

*The first look you see
may be while in a crowd.
It's subtly inviting.
It's message is loud.
It doesn't matter
what you try to do.
When you glance at her,
she's looking at you.*

*The next look you see
while the lights are down low.
Will tell you the thing
you've been wanting to know.
Don't get used to this look,
for it will pass soon.
It's precious but fleeting.
It's called the honeymoon.*

*Then comes the look
like the end of all time.
Her face will squint up
like she's sucked on a lime.
You may try to hold out
in spite of that stare.
She's used it since birth.
You don't have a prayer.*

*It's not a big secret
about all those looks.
You've heard it in songs
and read it in books.
Just do what she tells you
and brag when she cooks.
Then maybe you
will avoid the look.*

Misery

*Why do some people
just cause misery?
They look for evil
in all that they see.
They think that it's proper
to take from a man.
Then they will hurt him
as much as they can.*

*You found all you needed
in a library book.
You followed it carefully
in each step you took.
You'd wait 'til I'd settled
in for the night,
then you'd call the cops
and say we'd had a fight.*

*It didn't matter
what I had to say.
They took down your statement,
then hauled me away.
You planned it so carefully
and that's how it went.
And I would be guilty
'til proved innocent.*

*I didn't bother
to put up a fight,
for I believed
the system was right.
I listened as you told
your lies with such ease,
and knew you'd been prompted
for questions like these.*

*There isn't a chance
they'll charge perjury.
You said what they told you
with immunity.
You're a born liar
and you're really good.
The jury believed you,
so your charges stood.*

Gossip

It's only gossip, when it's about me.

Next

*Next: The word that I've dreaded.
I know that I'm headed
to the top of your "used to be" line.
Next: I know we are done.
Someone else is the one.
Now I'm going out of your mind.*

*Next: There once was a time,
I was waiting in line
to have my one chance with you.
Next: Now we're reaching the end.
Will my heart ever mend
or will I forever be blue?*

*Next: Now I'm learning the score.
You've just walked out the door
and I'm just a faint memory.
Next: Where do I go from here?
Will someone hold you near
and is there someone for me?*

*Next: I'll go on with my life.
You will not be my wife,
'cause you're not the marrying kind.
Next: Someone else holds my dream.
For now it must seem
that I've used up all my time.*

*Next: How this one word will haunt me.
Now I know that this won't be
a love that will last for all time.
Next: Is there one thing to do,
to prove that I love you
and get back in your waiting line.*

Tools

With the right tool, I can break anything.

One Sided Love

*Love so one sided's
a mystery to me.
If one is cheating,
the other should see.
Some give their all,
while others just take.
The heart loving blindly's
the one that will break.*

*I met a new friend
where we used to dance.
While we made small talk,
he mentioned romance.
He said just in passing
he'd been out with you.
Hiding my heart ache
took all I could do.*

*He didn't know
he had caused me such harm.
While I was struggling
to hide my alarm.
He changed the subject
to some other thing.
To him you were only
a casual fling.*

*He was with someone
and I could see.
She meant to him
what you mean to me.
They had been fighting
and while she was gone.
He wanted a shoulder
that he could cry on.*

*What is it that
is important to you.
Is there anything
else I can do,
to try and recapture
the times we once knew.
No one will love you
as much as I do.*

October

*October is that time of year
when seasons start to change.
The trees take on a different look,
and neighborhoods are strange.*

*City folk with well kept lawn,
becomes a country bumpkin.
For a time he decorates
with mums and straw and pumpkin.*

*Power drills hum and hammers bang
as gruesome scenes begin to hang.
Extra money has been spent
to pierce the night with fluorescent.*

*As if all this is not enough,
just as October's ending,
the parents send their kids around,
their arms with bags extending.*

*I sit there in my easy chair
and from it I'm not budgin'.
The kids call me a stubborn coot,
but I prefer curmudgeon.*

*Enjoy the season while it lasts,
for all too soon it will be past.
And then the time of sacrifice,
with freezing rain and snow and ice.*

It's our turn

*It's finally our turn.
We've waited so long,
for just the right person
to come along.
We've both had our share
of that which was wrong.
We've been tried and tested
and it made us strong.*

*I've never experienced
a love such as yours.
You're all I could wish for
and oh so much more.
I was ready to give up
that it could ever be.
Then God sent an angel
to return my heart to me.*

*I know now we're part
of a much greater plan.
You're why God made woman
to give to a man.
First we had lessons
that we had to learn,
now we are ready,
God's given our turn.*

*I know you're the woman
who was made for me.
I'll love you on earth
and eternity.
I've crossed all my rivers
and watched bridges burn,
but it was all worth it
to get to our turn.*

Students

*Attentive faces, shining bright
whet this old poet's appetite.
So much to tell, so little time,
to share my thoughts in words that rhyme.*

*If I could give one thing to you,
just be yourself in all you do.
Learn from all there is to see,
with now and then a thought of me.*

*There's more to you than you may know,
and every bit needs room to grow,
so feed your body, mind and soul,
'til all three parts make up the whole.*

*Take time for all God has in store,
to give life balance and much more.
Whatever comes, will be your gain,
though happiness, turmoil or pain.*

Outside

*I'll open my heart
and tell you how I feel.
I know you think you love me,
but I'm not sure it's real.
You're the only one I've been with,
but you cannot say the same.
For I've seen you with another
and I even know his name.*

*Now I'm standing on the outside,
looking in at all the fun.
I can see you're with another,
and I'm not your only one.
I know I shouldn't be here,
but I really need to know.
Just who it is you're seeing
and just where it is you go.*

*You were mine for just a moment
and the sweetest love I've known.
Now you say there's too much distance.
I've stood still while you have grown.
I'm the same as when you met me
and I don't expect to change.
It hurts to see you with another
and I even know his name.*

*Soon I will face the problem
that I've put off for so long.
I'll tell you all my secrets.
I know what's going on.
I fear that you will tell me
our love is not the same.
For I've seen you with another
and I even know his name.*

Suspenders

Behold the suspenders,
They're always in style.
Your belt needs assistance
after a while.
They're worn with tuxedoes,
or even blue jeans,
and say to the world,
you're a person of means.

So if you are nearing
that time in your life,
When keeping your pants up
is causing you strife,
consider suspenders
for extra support.
A fashion statement
or your last resort.

When you're with your lady,
you'll look very sleek.
She can pull your suspenders,
as you dance cheek to cheek.
If you give her a nickname,
that will be fine,
as long as you're careful,
and don't give her mine.

I call her Suspenders,
and everyone asks.
"Is it 'cause she supports you
In all your tasks?"
She came by that nickname
almost by chance.
I call her Suspenders
'cause she keeps up my pants.

The Test

*I'm really not unhappy
with this single life I chose.
Still I will change it all
if you accept what I propose.
You're not the first love that I've known
but I think you're the best,
so I offer you this simple test.*

*Do you love me? Please say yes.
Do you want me? Please say yes.
Will you be mine for all eternity?
Do you love me? Please say yes.
Do you want me? Please say yes.
Will you forsake all others just for me?*

*I thought that I could have my fun
and then be on my way.
I find your love is pulling me
in deeper every day.
That wanderlust is gone now.
You've put my heart to rest.
So please tell me that I have passed the test.*

*I'll be forever in your debt
if you accept my love.
I'll kiss the ground you walk on
and give thanks to God above.
Every day I spend with you,
I'll give my very best.
It starts as soon as you complete the test.*

Limerick of the Lady

I met a young lady of dance.
I knew I did not have a chance.
I tried anyway,
and I'm glad to say,
now everyday is romance.

Etherees

Each line has the same number of syllables as the line number.

Etheree of Man

It's
doubtful
I am now
half of the man
I thought I once was.
Did I fool myself then,
or does it seem better now?
Success is easy to review,
while failure is harder on the soul.
So maybe what I now think, never was.

Etheree to Poetry

*I
cannot
imagine
anything worse,
than having no rhyme
at the end of my verse.
It really isn't that hard
for a modern poetry bard.
Just give some thought of how to begin,
before you pick up your paper and pen.*

The Tomb

*He was hastily buried
as the Sabbath drew near.
No time to anoint him,
for the law then was clear.
With ointments and spices,
they drew near at dawn.
Then stood in amazement,
for the body was gone.*

*There were soldiers to guard him,
who now lay as dead.
Where once was his body,
stood an angel instead.
He had news for the mother
who grieved for her son.
"He's returned to the Father.
His work here is done".*

*They couldn't believe
the things they saw there.
They ran from the grave site,
their good news to share,
They had witnessed the wonder
of that first Easter dawn.
The tomb wasn't empty,
but the body was gone.*

*Proclaim to a lost world,
our savior still lives.
He was sacrificed for us
and eternal life gives.
There's little we must do,
this gift to receive.
Just ask for forgiveness.
In his name believe.*

*There's more to this story
that you need to know,
to carry the good news
wherever you go.
Read all about it
in Matthew through John,
how the tomb wasn't empty,
but the body was gone.*

Wall of Stone

Wall of stone,
built one piece at a time.
It's standing between
your heart and mine.
When we're together,
I feel so alone.
I can't get to you,
through this wall of stone.

We started with nothing
to keep us apart.
We planned for our future
and talked heart to heart.
But each time you hurt me
by running around.
You add one more stone
that I can't tear down.

Now there's a wall
between your heart and mine.
Walls don't just happen,
they're built over time.
Each time you hurt me,
you add to the pile.
And there'll be a strong wall
after a while.

Please tell me you'll help me
to tear down the wall.
If we work together,
I know it will fall.
Then we can start over
when our work is done.
With nothing between us
and two hearts as one.

Warm On The Outside

*She may be warm on the surface,
but so cold inside.
You can't always tell
what a smile has to hide.
With love there are chances
that you have to take.
Will it last forever,
or will your heart break.*

*The sun's shining brightly
and it looks so nice.
You'd think it was summer
if not for the ice.
As you're drawn into it,
the cold reaches you.
And you can't help remembering
a love you once knew.*

*She was warm on the outside,
but so cold within.
Her heart had been hardened
to not love again.
She was soft and inviting,
her face didn't show,
inside was a hard heart,
all covered with snow.*

*You always were honest
and open with her.
You had good intentions,
but she would infer,
that there was some evil
in all that you did.
She took all you gave her
and kept her heart hid.*

*Someone before you
had turned her to stone.
He promised forever,
then left her alone.
You thought you could reach her
where others had tried.
But she wouldn't trust you,
'cause someone else lied.*

*You're dressed for the weather,
'cause you've learned to live
with old mother nature
and all she can give.
But the only protection
is never to start,
with a soft, pretty woman
and a hard, frozen heart.*

*You wrap your arms 'round you
to shield from the cold.
But it comes from the inside,
as memories unfold.
Maybe you'll find another
and let go of the past.
But you'll always remember
that love may not last.*

Waitin'

I'm waitin'
'til the hurtin' goes away.
I'll probably find another,
but it won't be today.
I have a lot of love to give
and pretty soon I may.
I'm just waitin'
'til the hurtin' goes away.

When you first left,
I felt you took my world away with you.
Drinkin', thinkin', cryin',
was all that I could do.
Now I find your memory
growing fainter every day.
So if it takes a lifetime,
I know it will fade away.

It's not as bad as it once was.
I know there's hope for me.
At first when I would think of you,
it caused such misery.
Time has been a comfort,
though I still can feel the pain.
I know that one day soon
I'll find the strength to love again.

I've danced with lots of women
since day you set me free…
Some of them were all the things
a woman needs to be.
I know there's someone out there
just waitin' for the day.
That I can be there with them
when this hurtin' goes away.

We Need To Talk

*I answered the phone
'cause I knew it was you.
We started talking,
I hadn't a clue,
that while I was faithful,
to my honor bound,
you were out dancing
and running around.*

*We need to talk:
I no longer love you.
We need to talk:
I've found someone new.
Of all of the words
you will hear in your life.
"We need to talk"
will cut just like a knife.*

*You never gave me
any reason to doubt,
that you were faithful
when we were not out.
I either was with you
or I was alone.
The first I heard different
was over the phone.*

*I guess I will never learn
who I can trust.
I believe honor
and faith are a must.
If you love someone,
you have to believe,
they will give back
just what they receive.*

The words have been spoken,
we can't take them back.
I know you want something
that I seem to lack.
You may not find better,
but you have to look.
I think you'll find real men
are not like the book.

What is this?

What is this? What's happening to me?
This isn't how I used to be.
I tremble when I think of you,
and each day's exciting and new.

What is this that you've done to me?
Is this the way love is meant to be?
I want you, yet you scare me too.
I've given all I am to you.

Is there anything I can do,
to show you how I feel for you?
It can't be with these words alone.
Your love's more than I've ever known.

Do you feel the same about me?
Is that what's in your eyes I see
Reflection of love I have for you,
and knowing I'll always be true?

What's the Difference

When you think about it,
isn't it strange?
It's mostly the same parts,
just rearranged.
The difference is slight,
but no one denies,
it touches the heart
and pleases the eyes.

What is it about them
that turns us to mush.
The slightest of glances
can make our face flush.
If they show interest,
when we try to speak,
we feel our pulse quicken
and our knees go weak.

When you think about it,
the differences are few.
They're shaped slightly different
in one place or two.
But those subtle changes
are all that it takes,
to make men feel queasy
and give them the shakes.

It's obvious that someone
knew what to do,
to make the opposite
sex attract you.
It didn't just happen.
There must be a plan.
To make the woman
so appealing to man.

Why must you try to change me?

Why must you try to change me
into something that I'm not.
Am I the one you wanted,
or just the best you've got.
There's only been one perfect man
and he was not for you.
So take me as you find me
or tell me that we're through.

I'm standing in the shadows
of a love that used to be.
I thought you would be happy
and you only wanted me.
Now the gap that's come between us
grows wider every day,
and I'm standing on the sidelines
watching as you drift away.

This world you only visit
is the one in which I live.
I've tried to make you happy,
now there's nothing left to give.
It's true that we are different.
I could never be like you.
But we could be together
if our love was really true.

So now I'll stand here watching
as our love grows smaller still.
Perhaps you'll have a change of heart,
Lord knows I pray you will.
For now I'll keep on hoping
for a better remedy,
than standing, watching sadly
as you drift away from me.

You're the one I think of

*You're the one I think of
whenever she's gone.
You've always been the woman
that I could count on.
I'm sure that I will love her
for all eternity.
I'm sure that you will always
save some time for me.*

*Thanks for the dances
and the time that we shared.
I wouldn't be here
if I loved one who cared.
But until I can leave her
and go out on my own.
You're who I think of
whenever she's gone.*

*You're always there,
while she's dancing with me.
Watching from the sidelines
and wanting to be,
the one that I'm holding
and trying to please.
I know that you're waiting
for moments like these.*

*Maybe I'll see
what you know to be true.
That she doesn't love me
as much as you do.
'Til then we'll share moments
as they come along.
'Cause you're who I think of
whenever she's gone.*

The Man

I'm not the man I used to be, and probably never was.

Young

It's true, I'm as old as I've ever been,
but I'll never be this young again.
So if there is something I still want to do,
I had better get started,
and then see it through.

There may be a mountain I want to climb,
or maybe jot down a few lines that rhyme.
Perhaps there's a book somewhere in me,
or maybe a song
that yearns to be free.

It might be just a kind word or deed,
that I bring to someone
in their hour of need.
Maybe I'll show by the example I set,
a lesson in life my friends won't forget.

There is something special for everyone,
and if I don't do it, It might not get done.
Whatever it is, it's time to begin,
because I'll never be this young again.

Uncle Dan Bruffett
(October 29, 1921–December 9, 2004)

Who's the Whore?

As we were driving home one night,
and halted by a traffic light,
a lady stood with hose of mesh.
We knew at once her trade was flesh.

There was a look upon your face
that showed you held her in disgrace.
Is it because she's so direct
that causes you to lack respect?

She only has this one demand.
Before the love, it's cash in hand.
The lady is of ill repute,
that's not the cause of our dispute.

How much difference can there be?
Do you believe your love is free?
Everything I have is yours,
and yet you keep that list of chores.

It's always there so close at hand,
beside our bed on your night stand,
and every time I reach for you,
out comes that list of "honey do".

You tell me that I lack romance.
We never date or dine or dance.
But have you ever heard me say,
"Your chores aren't done, No love today"?

There's just two ways, or so I'm told,
love's either given or it's sold,
and whether it's for cash or chore,
you both sell love, so who's the whore?

Reducing Poetry

*(The last word of each line is reduced
by one letter)*

*I told the big bully to scram,
or my fist in his face I would cram.
He charged at me like a ram,
but who is still standing? I am.*

Leftover Limericks

There was a lady who kept score.
Her love she exchanged for a chore.
Although they were wed,
when she was in bed,
she was nothing more than a whore.

Her town and her name are the same.
She plays every man like a game.
Her name's Tulsa but,
reversed spells a slut,
and Tulsa lives up to her name.

Sweet potato isn't a yam,
anymore than steak is a ham.
So what's in a name?
You say they're the same.
I yam nothing more than I am.

A lady once thought she was hot,
but it became clear she was not.
She bathed every day,
with lotion and spray,
but wrinkled was all that she got.

This scene at the bank had been taped.
Her check bounced and she was a gaped.
He paid her to neck,
then wrote a bad check.
She cried "oh my gosh, I've been raped".

There once was a lady named May,
a virgin on her wedding day.
She never gave in,
to all the young men.
Too late, she found out she was gay.

*She's skinny as a girl can be,
but still counts every calorie.
She won't take a bite,
unless is says "light".
Sometimes she's not easy to see.*

*You seem to think you have the right
to change the words that I recite.
Before you begin
to use your red pen.
You'd better get ready to fight.*

*There once was a lady of class,
who married a man, mean and crass.
The child that they had,
is just like his dad.
He's called the neighborhood jackass.*

*She weighs a ton, or more than that,
but thinks she's as light as a gnat.
She tries to squeeze in
clothes made for the thin,
but they just push out all the fat.*

*The lady tried her very best.
But just wasn't up to the test.
A man would ask please.
Then weak in the knees.
Do I have to tell you the rest?*

*I sit here with paper and pen.
I don't know where I should begin.
I know it must rhyme,
but that takes more time.
So maybe I'll fake it 'til then.*

About the Author

Douglas Bruffett is an award-winning and internationally published poet. Now retired, he resides on Caney Lake near Chatham, Louisiana, with his wife, Beth.

978-0-595-38535-5
0-595-38535-4

Printed in the United States
47507LVS00007B/82